To:

_____

From:

_____

Date:

_____

# PROMISES & PRAYERS

## A Family Christmas

FAMILY
CHRISTIAN
PRESS

# PROMISES & PRAYERS

## A Family Christmas

FAMILY CHRISTIAN PRESS
Grand Rapids, MI 49530

ISBN 1-58334-146-3

*The quoted ideas expressed in this book (but not scripture verses) are not, in
all cases, exact quotations, as some have been edited for clarity and brevity.
In all cases, the author has attempted to maintain the speaker's original
intent. In some cases, quoted material for this book was obtained from
secondary sources, primarily print media. While every effort was made to
ensure the accuracy of these sources, the accuracy cannot be guaranteed. For
additions, deletions, corrections or clarifications in future editions of this
text, please write FAMILY CHRISTIAN PRESS.*

Certain elements of this text, including quotations, stories, and selected
groupings of Bible verses, have appeared, in part or in whole, in
publications produced by Brighton Books of Nashville, TN; these excerpts
are used with permission.

Scripture taken from the HOLY BIBLE, NEW INTERNATIONAL
VERSION ©. NIV ©. Copyright © 1973, 1978, 1984, by International
Bible Society. Used by permission of Zondervan Publishing House. All
rights reserved.

Scripture taken from THE MESSAGE. Copyright © 1993,
1994,1995,1996. Used by permission of NavPress Publishing Group.

Scripture taken from the NEW AMERICAN STANDARD BIBLE®,
Copyright © 1960, 1962, 1963, 1968, 1971, 1972, 1973, 1975, 1977,
1995 by The Lockman Foundation. Used by permission.

Printed in the United States of America
Cover Design & Page Layout: *Bart Dawson*

1 2 3 4 5 6 7 8 9 10 • 02 03 04 05 06 07 08 09 10

*For Families Everywhere...*

*May God's Peace*
*Be With You Always.*

# Table of Contents

❧❧❧❧❧❧❧❧❧❧❧❧❧❧❧❧❧❧❧❧❧❧❧❧❧❧❧❧❧❧❧❧❧❧❧❧❧❧❧❧❧❧❧❧

*I*t's Christmastime, and there is so much to do: meals to cook, parties to plan, and presents to wrap. Sometimes, amid the crush of holiday plans, we may be tempted to forget, at least temporarily, the One whose birth we celebrate. But as Christians, our most important obligation is clear: We must offer our prayers and our praise to God and to His Son.

The holiday season provides many families with the opportunity to gather together and offer thanks to the Giver of all things good. This book is intended to remind family members of all ages that God's promises are everlasting and that His grace is given freely to those who accept His Son into their hearts.

Each chapter of this text is a collection of Bible verses and inspirational quotations from notable Christian thinkers, and each chapter concludes with a prayer. Readers are encouraged to share these pages with family members and friends.

The Christmas holidays are, of course, a time when Christians around the world celebrate the birth of Jesus. May we, as believers, never allow the demands of the season to obscure the real reason for our celebration: the coming of our Savior.

❧❧❧❧❧❧❧❧❧❧❧❧❧❧❧❧❧❧❧❧❧❧❧❧❧❧❧❧❧❧❧❧❧❧❧❧❧❧❧❧❧❧❧❧

# The Promise of Christmas

For God so loved the world, that he gave
his only begotten Son . . . .

—*John 3:16 KJV*

*T*wo thousand years ago, in the village of Bethlehem, God fulfilled His promise by sending His Son into this world so that those who open their hearts to Him might have eternal life. Each year, as the Christmas season nears, Christians focus their thoughts and prayers on the One whose birth they celebrate: Christ Jesus.

Thomas Brooks spoke for believers of every generation when he observed, "Christ is the sun, and all the watches of our lives should be set by the dial of his motion." Christ, indeed, is the ultimate Savior of mankind and the personal Savior of those who believe in Him. As His servants, we should place Him at the very center of our lives, not only on Christmas day, but also on every day of the year.

God has made His promise clear. When we accept God's Son and accept God's grace, then we will receive life abundant and eternal. And that, of course, is God's Christmas gift to the world, a gift of love that is infinite, unshakable, unchanging, and eternal.

In the beginning was the Word, and the Word was with God, and the Word was God . . . . And the Word was made flesh, and dwelt among us, (and we beheld his glory, the glory as of the only begotten of the Father) full of grace and truth.

—*John 1:1,14 KJV*

❄

The Father loveth the Son, and hath given all things into his hand. He that believeth on the Son hath everlasting life . . . .

—*John 3:35-36 KJV*

❄

Jesus Christ founded His Kingdom on the weakest link of all: a Baby.

—*Oswald Chambers*

Let us remember that the Christmas heart is a giving heart, a wide-open heart that thinks of others first. The birth of the baby Jesus stands as the most significant event in all history because it has meant the pouring into a sick world of the healing medicine of love which has transformed all manner of hearts for almost two thousand years.

—*George Matthew Adams*

O Sovereign God! You have humbled yourself in order to exalt us. You became poor so that we might become rich. You came to us so that we might come to you. You took upon yourself our humanity in order to raise us up into eternal life. All this comes through your grace, free and unmerited, all this through your beloved Son, our Lord and Savior, Jesus Christ.

—*Karl Barth*

If only we would stop lamenting and look up. God is here. Christ is risen. The Spirit has been poured out from on high.

—*A. W. Tozer*

In every Christian, Christ lives again. Every true believer is a return to first-century Christianity.

—*Vance Havner*

All hail the power of Jesus' name! Let angels prostrate fall; bring forth the royal diadem, and crown Him Lord of all . . . .

—*Edward Perronet*

*Away in a manger,*
*no crib for a bed,*
*The little Lord Jesus lay*
*down his sweet head.*
*The stars in the sky looked*
*down where he lay,*
*The little Lord Jesus,*
*asleep on the hay.*

*The cattle are lowing,*
*the baby awakes,*
*But little Lord Jesus,*
*no crying he makes.*
*I love Thee, Lord Jesus!*
*Look down from the sky,*
*And stand by my cradle till*
*morning is nigh.*

—

ANONYMOUS

*I am come that they might have
life, and that they might
have it more abundantly.*

—

JOHN 10:10 KJV

*I am the good shepherd:
the good shepherd giveth his life
for the sheep.*

—

JOHN 10:11 KJV

## A Prayer at Christmas

Lord, I thank You for the gift of Your Son,
and I thank You for this season of celebration.
Let me keep the love of Jesus in my heart,
and let me celebrate His birth by sharing
His Good News with my family,
with my friends, and with all
who cross my path.

*Amen*

# A Family Christmas

Above all, love each other deeply.

—*1 Peter 4:8 NIV*

*C*hristmas is a season when families gather together and share food, songs, stories, and memories. Holiday celebrations bring us together, and holiday traditions remind us of our heritage.

Christmas is a time for going home. And even if we can't enjoy the physical presence of family and friends, we can find a special place for them in our hearts.

This holiday season, like every other, should be a time of thanksgiving and fellowship. And, amid the holiday happenings, let us always remember the One whose birth we celebrate. Jesus said, "Just as the Father has loved Me, I have also loved you; abide in My love" (John 15:9 NASB). He first loved us; let us return His love by sharing it.

Surely Christmas is the very best time of the year to be home with loved ones.

—*W. Herschel Ford*

❄

What can you do for this world? Go home and love your family.

—*Mother Teresa*

❄

A happy family is but an earlier heaven.

—*Sir John Browing*

The secret of a happy home life is that the members of the family learn to give and receive love.

—*Billy Graham*

It is a reverent thing to see an ancient castle or building not in decay, or to see a fair timber tree sound and perfect. How much more beautiful it is to behold an ancient and noble family that has stood against the waves and weathers of time.

—*Francis Bacon*

The family circle is the supreme conductor of Christianity.

—*Henry Drummond*

>>>

*A Christmas family-party!*
*We know of nothing in nature*
*more delightful!*

—

CHARLES DICKENS

>>>>>>>>>>>>>>>>>>>>>>>>>>>>>>>>>>>>>>>>>>>>>>>>>

## A Prayer at Christmas

Dear Lord, I am blessed to be part of
the family of God where I find love and
acceptance. You have also blessed me with
my earthly family. During this Christmas
season and throughout the year, let me show
the same love and acceptance for my own
family that You have shown for me.

*Amen*

# The Christmas Story

Glory to God in the highest, and on earth
peace, good will toward men.

—*Luke 2:14 KJV*

The Christmas Story begins in a far-away land: a babe is born, the angels rejoice, and the world is forever changed.

❄

And it came to pass in those days, that there went out a decree from Caesar Augustus, that all the world should be taxed.... And all went to be taxed, every one into his own city. And Joseph also went up from Galilee, out of the city of Nazareth, into Judea, unto the city of David, which is called Bethlehem, (because he was of the house and lineage of David) to be taxed with Mary his espoused wife, being great with child. And so it was, that, while they were there, the days were accomplished that she should be delivered. And she brought forth her firstborn son, and wrapped him in swaddling clothes, and laid him in a manger; because there was no room for them in the inn. And there were in the same country shepherds abiding in the field, keeping watch over their flock by night. And, lo, the angel of the Lord came upon them, and the glory of the Lord shone round about them; and they were sore afraid. And the angel said unto them, Fear not: for, behold, I bring you good tidings of great joy, which shall be to all people. For unto you is born this day in the city of David a Saviour, which is Christ the Lord. And this shall be a sign unto you; Ye shall find the babe wrapped in swaddling clothes, lying in a manger. And suddenly there was with the angel a multitude of the heavenly host praising God, and saying, Glory to God in the highest, and on earth peace, good will toward men.

—*Luke 2:1-14 KJV*

❖❖❖❖❖❖❖❖❖❖❖❖❖❖❖❖❖❖❖❖❖❖❖❖❖❖❖❖❖❖❖❖❖❖❖❖❖❖❖❖❖❖❖❖❖❖

The birth of Jesus is the sunrise in the Bible.

*—Henry Van Dyke*

The simple shepherds heard the voice of an angel and found their Lamb; the wise men saw the light of a star and found their Wisdom.

*—Fulton Sheen*

Let us pray that we shall be able to welcome Jesus at Christmas—not in the cold manger of our heart, but in a heart full of love and humanity.

*—Mother Teresa*

❖❖❖❖❖❖❖❖❖❖❖❖❖❖❖❖❖❖❖❖❖❖❖❖❖❖❖❖❖❖❖❖❖❖❖❖❖❖❖❖❖❖❖❖❖❖

✧✧✧✧✧✧✧✧✧✧✧✧✧✧✧✧✧✧✧✧✧✧✧✧✧✧✧✧✧✧✧✧✧✧✧✧✧✧✧✧✧✧✧✧✧✧✧

*Christmas, like God,*
*is timeless and eternal.*

—

DALE EVANS

✧✧✧✧✧✧✧✧✧✧✧✧✧✧✧✧✧✧✧✧✧✧✧✧✧✧✧✧✧✧✧✧✧✧✧✧✧✧✧✧✧✧✧✧✧✧✧

*A Prayer at Christmas*

Thank You, Lord, for the gift of Your Son
Jesus. During this season when we celebrate
His birth, let my love for Christ be reflected
in my words, my thoughts, and my deeds.
And throughout the year, let me share
His transforming message with a world
in need of His love and His peace.

*Amen*

# The Meaning of Christmas

And we have seen and testify that the Father has sent his Son to be the Savior of the world.

—1 John 4:14 NIV

No amount of commercialism or fanfare should obscure the fact that Christmastime is the annual birthday party of the Christian faith. Christmas day is, first and forever, a religious holiday—a time for Christians everywhere to rejoice, to pray, and to give heartfelt thanks.

Noted theologian Karl Barth observed, "Today, the Christmas message is delivered—the message of the light of the world which breaks through from above, always from above . . . ."

During this time of Christmas, it is proper that we keep our eyes and our hearts lifted upwards, always upwards, as we joyfully celebrate the reason for the Christmas season: Christ Jesus.

*The magic message of Christmas is that God gave us so much more than we can possibly give back!*

—

NORMAN VINCENT PEALE

Are you willing to believe that love is the strongest thing in the world—stronger than hate, stronger than evil, stronger than death, and that the blessed life which began in Bethlehem nineteen hundred years ago is the image and brightness of the Eternal Love? Then you can keep Christmas.

—*Henry Van Dyke*

Christmas means the beginning of Christianity—and a second chance for the world.

—*Peter Marshall*

The work of Jesus is the creation of saints.

—*Oswald Chambers*

*For the Son of man
is come to seek and to save
that which was lost.*

—

LUKE 19:10 KJV

*O little town of Bethlehem,*
*How still we see thee lie,*
*Above thy deep and*
*dreamless sleep,*
*The silent stars go by;*
*Yet in thy dark streets shineth*
*The everlasting Light,*
*The hopes and fears*
*of all the years*
*Are met in thee tonight.*

*O holy Child of Bethlehem!*
*Descend to us we pray;*
*Cast out our sin and enter in,*
*Be born in us today.*
*We hear the Christmas angels*
*The great glad tidings tell;*
*O come to us abide with us,*
*Our Lord Emmanuel!*

—

PHILLIPS BROOKS, 1867

The Christmas message is that there is hope for humanity, hope of pardon, hope of peace with God, hope of glory.

—*J. I. Packer*

The Christmas story gives its triumphant answer: "Be not afraid."

—*Karl Barth*

>>>

*The whole meaning of Christmas can be summed up in the miracle of Christ's birth.*

—

ARTHUR BRYANT

>>>>>>>>>>>>>>>>>>>>>>>>>>>>>>>>>>>>>>>>>>>>>>>>>

✧✧✧✧✧✧✧✧✧✧✧✧✧✧✧✧✧✧✧✧✧✧✧✧✧✧✧✧✧✧✧✧✧✧✧✧✧✧✧✧✧✧✧✧✧

# A Prayer at Christmas

Lord, the holiday season can be a time of busyness and distractions. Keep me mindful, Father, of the true meaning of Christmas, and let me share Christ's love and His message with my family, with my friends, and with the world. Make me a faithful servant of Your Son on Christmas day *and* every day of my life.

## Amen

✧✧✧✧✧✧✧✧✧✧✧✧✧✧✧✧✧✧✧✧✧✧✧✧✧✧✧✧✧✧✧✧✧✧✧✧✧✧✧✧✧✧✧✧✧

*A Time for Celebration*

This is the day which the LORD hath made; we will rejoice and be glad in it.

*—Psalm 118:24 KJV*

*O*swald Chambers correctly observed, "Joy is the great note all throughout the Bible." C. S. Lewis echoed that thought when he wrote, "Joy is the serious business of heaven." But, even the most dedicated Christians can, on occasion, forget to celebrate each day for what it is: a priceless gift from God.

During this holiday season, let us be cheerful Christians with smiles on our faces and kind words on our lips. After all, this is the season that we celebrate the birth of God's Son. We are commanded to rejoice and be glad. And, with no further ado, let the celebration begin . . . .

Christmas is the season of joy, of holiday greetings exchanged, of gift-giving, and of families united.

*—Norman Vincent Peale*

Would that Christmas lasted the whole year through (as it ought).

*—Charles Dickens*

Christmas goes on and on as it always does and always will, forever and ever and ever.

*—Pearl Buck*

Let the hearts of those who seek the Lord rejoice. Look to the Lord and his strength; seek his face always.

*—1 Chronicles 16:10-11 NIV*

Rejoice evermore. Pray without ceasing. In every thing give thanks: for this is the will of God in Christ Jesus concerning you.

*—1 Thessalonians 5:16-18 KJV*

Delight thyself also in the LORD; and he shall give thee the desires of thine heart.

*—Psalm 37:4 KJV*

❖❖❖❖❖❖❖❖❖❖❖❖❖❖❖❖❖❖❖❖❖❖❖❖❖❖❖❖❖❖❖❖❖❖❖❖❖❖❖❖❖❖❖❖❖

Joy is available to all who seek His riches. The key to joy is found in the person of Jesus Christ and in His will.

*—Kay Arthur*

❄

In the great orchestra we call life, you have an instrument and a song, and you owe it to God to play them both sublimely.

*—Max Lucado*

❄

When the dream of our heart is one that God has planted there, a strange happiness flows into us. At that moment, all of the spiritual resources of the universe are released to help us. Our praying is then at one with the will of God and becomes a channel for the Creator's purposes for us and our world.

*—Catherine Marshall*

❖❖❖❖❖❖❖❖❖❖❖❖❖❖❖❖❖❖❖❖❖❖❖❖❖❖❖❖❖❖❖❖❖❖❖❖❖❖❖❖❖❖❖❖❖

*A Prayer at Christmas*

Holy, Holy, Holy . . . You are a righteous
and holy God, and I rejoice in You.
Renew a right spirit within me, Father,
and let me serve You and obey the teachings
of Your Word. Make this Christmas season
a time of worship, a time of celebration,
and a time of praise for Your Son.

*Amen*

# A Time for Friends

A friend loveth at all times.

—*Proverbs 17:17 KJV*

$\mathcal{F}$riend: a one-syllable word describing "a person who is attached to another by feelings of affection or personal regard." This definition, or one very similar to it, can be found in any dictionary, but genuine friendship is much more. When we examine the deeper meaning of friendship, so many descriptors come to mind: trustworthiness, loyalty, helpfulness, kindness, understanding, forgiveness, encouragement, humor, and cheerfulness, to mention but a few.

Genuine friendship should be treasured and nurtured, especially during the holiday season. As Christians, we are commanded to love one another. This holiday season and throughout the year, let us resolve to be trustworthy, encouraging, loyal friends. Friendship is, after all, a glorious gift, praised by God. May we give thanks for that gift and nurture it.

Christmas is a together time.

—*Charles Schulz*

❄

Give yourself at Christmas; there really is no more wonderful gift.

—*Dorothy Wilson*

❄

A friend is a present you give yourself.

—*Robert Louis Stevenson*

*A Christmas gift symbolizes the love that Christians bear to one another, in the name of the One who loved them all.*

—

DONALD CULROSS PEATTIE

*For I am persuaded, that neither death, nor life, nor angels, nor principalities, nor powers, nor things present, nor things to come, nor height, nor depth, nor any other creature, shall be able to separate us from the love of God, which is in Christ Jesus our Lord.*

—

ROMANS 8:38-39 KJV

# A Prayer at Christmas

Lord, You seek abundance and joy for me
and for all of Your children. One way that
I can share Your joy is through the gift of
friendship. Help me to be a loyal friend, Lord.
Let me be ready to listen, ready to encourage,
and ready to offer a helping hand. Keep me
mindful that I am a servant of Your Son Jesus.
Let me be a worthy servant, Lord, and
a worthy friend. And, may the love
of Jesus shine through me
today and forever.

*Amen*

# Peace on Earth

These things I have spoken unto you,
that in me ye might have peace.

—*John 16:33 KJV*

*P*eace on earth . . . the words are so familiar and yet so elusive. During the holiday season, we pray for peace in our own lives and for peace throughout the world.

When we seek to discover peace through our own means, we inevitably fall short, both as individuals and as nations. But, when we turn our thoughts, our hopes, and our prayers to the One who slept in the manger, He offers us the only peace that endures: His.

Jesus offers us peace, not as the world gives, but as He alone gives. We, as believers, can accept His peace or ignore it. When we accept the peace of Jesus Christ into our hearts, our lives are transformed and the promise of the Christmas season is fulfilled.

*I heard the bells on
Christmas Day,
Their old familiar carols play,
And wild and sweet
Their words repeat
Of peace on earth,
good-will to men!*

—

HENRY WADSWORTH LONGFELLOW

*Silent Night! Holy Night!*
*All is calm, all is bright.*
*Round yon virgin*
*mother and child!*
*Holy infant so tender and mild,*
*Sleep in heavenly peace,*
*Sleep in heavenly peace.*

*Silent Night! Holy Night!*
*Shepherds quake at the sight!*
*Glories stream from heaven afar,*
*Heavenly hosts sing Alleluia!*
*Christ the Savior is born!*
*Christ the Savior is born!*

—

FATHER JOSEPH MOHR, 1818

Peace with God is where all peace begins.

—*Jim Gallery*

Like a spring of pure water, God's peace in our hearts brings cleansing and refreshment to our minds and bodies.

—*Billy Graham*

Look around you and you'll be distressed; look within yourself and you'll be depressed; look at Jesus, and you'll be at rest!

—*Corrie ten Boom*

That peace, which has been described and which believers enjoy, is a participation of the peace which their glorious Lord and Master himself enjoys.

*—Jonathan Edwards*

❄

O God, Thou hast made us for Thyself, and our hearts are restless until they find their rest in Thee.

*—Saint Augustine*

❄

And so, at this Christmastime, I greet you. Not quite as the world sends greetings, but with the prayer that for you, now and forever, the day breaks and shadows flee away.

*—Fra Giovanni*

*As fits the holy
Christmas birth,
Be this, good friends,
our carol still—
Be peace on earth,
be peace on earth,
To men of gentle will.*

—

WILLIAM MAKEPEACE THACKERAY

*Peace I leave with you,
my peace I give unto you:
not as the world giveth,
give I unto you. Let not
your heart be troubled,
neither let it be afraid.*

—

JOHN 14:27 KJV

## A Prayer at Christmas

Heavenly Father, when I turn my thoughts
and my prayers to Your Son, I am blessed.
On these days when I celebrate Christ's birth,
let me welcome Him into my heart, and
let me accept His peace, not just for today,
but for all eternity.

### Amen

# A Season of Good Cheer

The cheerful heart has a continual feast.

*Proverbs 15:15 NIV*

The holiday season offers many opportunities to celebrate with family and friends. But sometimes, amid the rush to meet Christmas deadlines, we don't always feel much like celebrating. To the contrary, we may feel overwhelmed.

When we fret over Christmas, instead of savoring it, we must redirect our thoughts and our prayers to the One whose birth and resurrection forever transformed the world.

The Christian life is a cause for celebration. Christ promises us lives of abundance, wholeness, and joy, but He does not force His joy upon us. We must claim His promises for ourselves, and when we do, Jesus, in turn, fills our spirits with His power and His love. Then, as God's children, we can share Christ's joy as we share His love. By doing so, we experience the true meaning of Christmas.

*If you can keep Christmas
for a day,
why not always?*

—

HENRY VAN DYKE

May the God of hope fill you with all joy and peace as you trust in him, so that you may overflow with hope by the power of the Holy Spirit.

—*Romans 15:13 NIV*

Make a joyful noise unto the LORD, all ye lands. Serve the LORD with gladness: come before his presence with singing.

—*Psalm 100:1-2 KJV*

Christmas day is a day of joy and charity. May God make you very rich in both.

—*Phillips Brooks*

Then let every heart keep Christmas within. Christ's pity for sorrow, Christ's hatred for sin, Christ's care for the weakest, Christ's courage for right, Everywhere, everywhere, Christmas tonight!

—*Phillips Brooks*

It is good to be children sometimes, and never better than at Christmas, when its mighty Founder was a child himself.

—*Charles Dickens*

*Let's not permit the crowds
and the rush to crowd Christmas
out of our hearts . . .
for that's where it belongs.*

—

PETER MARSHALL

But it is good for me to draw near to God: I have put my trust in the Lord GOD.

*—Psalm 73:28 KJV*

Trust in the LORD with all thine heart; and lean not unto thine own understanding. In all thy ways acknowledge him, and he shall direct thy paths.

*—Proverbs 3:5-6 KJV*

Let not your heart be troubled: ye believe in God, believe also in me.

*—John 14:1 KJV*

## A Prayer at Christmas

Dear Lord, during this holiday season and
throughout the year, You give me so many
reasons to celebrate. Today, let me choose
an attitude of cheerfulness. Let me be a joyful
Christian, Lord, quick to smile, quick
to laugh, and quick to forgive. Let me share
Your goodness with all whom I meet so
that Your love might shine in me
and through me.

## Amen

# A Time of Thanksgiving

I will give thanks to the LORD with all my heart; I will tell of all Your wonders. I will be glad and exult in You; I will sing praise to Your name, O Most High.

*—Psalm 9:1-2 NASB*

*We,* as believing Christians, are truly blessed beyond measure. During the Christmas season, we pause to give thanks to our Creator for the gift of His Son. When we slow down and express our gratitude to the One who made us, we enrich our own lives and the lives of those around us.

Thanksgiving should never be reserved for a single day or a single season of the year. Instead, thanksgiving should become a habit, a regular part of our daily routines. God has blessed us in miraculous ways, and we owe Him everything, including our never-ending praise.

Give thanks in all circumstances; for this is God's will for you in Christ Jesus.

*—1 Thessalonians 5:18 NIV*

And let the peace of God rule in your hearts . . . and be ye thankful.

*—Colossians 3:15 KJV*

Thanks be to God for his indescribable gift!

*—2 Corinthians 9:15 NIV*

I realized that songs, good feelings, beautiful liturgies, nice presents, big dinners, and many sweet words do not make Christmas. Christmas is saying yes to something beyond all emotions and feelings. Christmas is saying yes to a hope based on God's initiative. Christmas is believing that the salvation of the world is God's work, and not mine.

—*Henri Nouwen*

The only real blind person at Christmastime is he who has not Christmas in his heart.

—*Helen Keller*

It is only with gratitude that life becomes rich.

—*Dietrich Bonhoeffer*

Why wait until the fourth Thursday in November? Why wait until the morning of December twenty-fifth? Thanksgiving to God should be an everyday affair. The time to be thankful is now!

*—Jim Gallery*

Christmas is a good time to take stock of our blessings.

*—Pat Boone*

Praise ye the LORD. O give thanks unto the LORD; for he is good: for his mercy endureth for ever.

*—Psalm 106:1 KJV*

# A Prayer at Christmas

Lord, Your gifts are beyond my
comprehension. May I live each day
with thanksgiving in my heart and praise
on my lips. Thank You for the gift
of Your Son and for the promise
of eternal life. During this season,
let me share the joyous news
of Jesus' birth, and let my life be
a testimony to His love
and to His grace.

*Amen*

# And the Greatest of These Is Love

But now abide faith, hope, love, these three; but the greatest of these is love.

—*1 Corinthians 13:13 NASB*

God is love, and the birthday celebration of God's Son is a time when love should fill our hearts. Christmas is a season for sharing feelings of warmth and appreciation with family members and friends.

Let us gather together and make this holiday season a time to express genuine love and affection for all who cross our paths. When we do, we make ourselves dutiful servants of the One whose birth is the reason for this glorious season.

Christmas is most truly Christmas when we celebrate it by giving the light of love to those who need it most.

*—Ruth Carter Stapleton*

If we love one another, God abides in us, and His love is perfected in us.

*—1 John 4:12 NASB*

A new commandment I give unto you, That ye love one another; as I have loved you . . . .

*—John 13:34 KJV*

I tell you the truth, whatever you did for one of the least of these brothers of mine, you did for me.

—*Matthew 25:40 NIV*

Christmas, my child, is love in action. Every time we love, every time we give, it's Christmas.

—*Dale Evans*

There are all kinds of presents one can get for Christmas. The best is love.

—*Helen Hayes*

*Honor all men.*
*Love the brotherhood.*
*Fear God.*
*Honor the king.*

—

*1 PETER 2:17 KJV*

*Since love grows within you,
so beauty grows.
For love is
the beauty of the soul.*

—

SAINT AUGUSTINE

If Jesus is the preeminent One in our lives, then we will love each other, submit to each other, and treat one another fairly in the Lord.

—*Warren Wiersbe*

The whole being of any Christian is Faith and Love. Faith brings the man to God; love brings him to men.

—*Martin Luther*

## A Prayer at Christmas

Lord, during this season when we celebrate
the birth of Your Son, help me to show
kindness to all those who cross my path,
and let me show tenderness and unfailing love
to my family and friends. Make me generous
with words of encouragement and praise.
And, help me always to reflect the love that
Christ Jesus gives to me so that through me,
others might find Him.

*Amen*

# A Time for Prayer

Rejoice evermore. Pray without ceasing.
In every thing give thanks: for this is the will
of God in Christ Jesus concerning you.

—*1 Thessalonians 5:16-18 KJV*

On Christmas day—and every other— we are called by God to offer our prayers to Him. When we weave the habit of prayer into the very fabric of our days, we invite our Creator to become a partner in every aspect of our lives. When we consult God on an hourly basis, we avail ourselves of His wisdom, His strength, and His love.

We must never limit our prayers to meals or to bedtime. And, we must never reserve our prayers for a particular season of the year. Instead, we should pray constantly about things great and small. God is listening, and He wants to hear from us. Now.

Don't pray when you feel like it; make an appointment with the King and keep it.

—*Corrie ten Boom*

❄

He who kneels most stands best.

—*D. L. Moody*

❄

Prayer should not be regarded as a duty which must be performed, but rather as a privilege to be enjoyed, a rare delight that is always revealing some new beauty.

—*E. M. Bounds*

❄

I live in the spirit of prayer; I pray as I walk, when I lie down, and when I rise. And, the answers are always coming.

—*George Mueller*

The effective prayer of a righteous man can accomplish much.

*—James 5:16 NASB*

Watch ye therefore, and pray always . . . .

*—Luke 21:36 KJV*

Ask and it shall be given to you; seek and you shall find; knock and it shall be opened to you. For every one who asks receives, and he who seeks finds, and to him who knocks it shall be opened.

*—Matthew 7:7-8 NASB*

The only way to pray is to pray; and the way to pray well is to pray much.

*—Henri Nouwen*

In souls filled with love, the desire to please God is continual prayer.

*—John Wesley*

Pray, and let God worry.

*—Martin Luther*

In the New Testament, prayer is based on a relationship with God through Jesus Christ.

—*Oswald Chambers*

When we entrust our requests to him, we trust him to honor our prayers with holy judgment.

—*Max Lucado*

Prayer is our privilege of constant, unbroken communication with God.

—*Shirley Dobson*

❖❖❖❖❖❖❖❖❖❖❖❖❖❖❖❖❖❖❖❖❖❖❖❖❖❖❖❖❖❖❖❖❖❖❖❖❖❖❖❖❖❖❖❖❖❖

The best and sweetest flowers of Paradise God gives to his people when they are upon their knees. Prayer is the gate of heaven, a key to let us into Paradise.

—*Thomas Brooks*

✺

Prayer: the key of the day and the lock of the night.

—*Thomas Fuller*

✺

God is always listening.

—*Stormie Omartian*

❖❖❖❖❖❖❖❖❖❖❖❖❖❖❖❖❖❖❖❖❖❖❖❖❖❖❖❖❖❖❖❖❖❖❖❖❖❖❖❖❖❖❖❖❖❖

# A Prayer at Christmas

Heavenly Father, during this season, as we
celebrate the birth of Jesus, keep me mindful
that Christmas is a time for thanksgiving
and prayer. I pray to You, Father, because
You desire it and because I need it.
Prayer not only changes things; it also changes
me. Make me a prayerful Christian, Lord,
and let me turn every aspect of my life
over to You, today and forever.

## Amen

# A Time for Praise

I will praise thee with my whole heart....
—*Psalm 138:1 KJV*

When is the best time to praise God? On Christmas Day? Before dinner is served? In church? When we tuck little children into bed? None of the above. The best time to praise God is all day, every day, to the greatest extent we can, with thanksgiving in our hearts and with a song on our lips.

Theologian Wayne Oates once admitted, "Many of my prayers are made with my eyes open. You see, it seems I'm always praying about something, and it's not always convenient—or safe—to close my eyes." Dr. Oates understood that God always hears our prayers and that the relative position of our eyelids is of no concern to Him.

During this glorious celebration of Christ's birth, let us praise Him without ceasing. When we do, we welcome the babe of Bethlehem into our hearts, which, by the way, is exactly where He belongs.

*O come, all ye faithful,*
*joyful and triumphant;*
*O come, let us adore Him,*
*Christ the Lord!*

—

JOHN FRANCIS WADE

Bethlehem's child was sent to us as a human being through an Incarnation that we cannot explain, the birth embodied a dimension of God that we probably would not have understood otherwise. God thought so much of us that God wanted to be one of us, to hold us close. Such sheer grace is the theme of Christmas.

—*Edgar R. Trexler*

God shares himself generously and graciously.

—*Eugene Peterson*

Is anyone happy? Let him sing songs of praise.

*—James 5:13 NIV*

The LORD is my strength and song, and He
has become my salvation; He is my God, and I
will praise Him.

*—Exodus 15:2 NIV*

I will praise the name of God with a song,
and will magnify him with thanksgiving.

*—Psalm 69:30 KJV*

# A Prayer at Christmas

Lord, I praise You for the gift of the Christ
child and for the gift of Your love. Your hand
created the smallest grain of sand and the
grandest stars in the heavens. You watch over
Your entire creation, and You watch over me.
I will praise You, Father, throughout this
Christmas season and throughout eternity.

## Amen

# A Time for Generosity

God loves a cheerful giver.

—2 Corinthians 9:7 NIV

Christmas is the season for giving, but gift-giving need not be synonymous with commercialism. The holiday season is the perfect time to share spiritual gifts as well as material ones. Spiritual gifts, of course, should take priority, but we must also give freely of our possessions, especially to those in need.

The words of Jesus are unambiguous: "Freely you have received, freely give" (Matthew 10:8 NIV). May this holiday season, and every one hereafter, be a time when we, as followers of Christ, show our love for Him through our generosity to others.

Material gifts are always secondary to spiritual gifts.

—*Rose Kennedy*

We must not only give what we have, we must also give what we are.

—*Désiré Joseph Mercier*

To celebrate the heart of Christmas is to forget ourselves in the service of others.

—*Henry C. Link*

Carry each other's burdens, and in this way you will fulfill the law of Christ.

*—Galatians 6:2 NIV*

And above all things have fervent charity among yourselves: for charity shall cover the multitude of sins.

*—1 Peter 4:8 KJV*

Let us not become weary in doing good, for at the proper time we will reap a harvest if we do not give up.

*—Galatians 6:9 NIV*

❖❖❖❖❖❖❖❖❖❖❖❖❖❖❖❖❖❖❖❖❖❖❖❖❖❖❖❖❖❖❖❖❖❖❖❖❖❖❖❖❖❖❖❖❖❖

And above all these things put on charity, which is the bond of perfectness.

*—Colossians 3:14 KJV*

As we have therefore opportunity, let us do good unto all men, especially unto them who are of the household of faith.

*—Galatians 6:10 KJV*

Blessed is he that considereth the poor.

*—Psalm 41:1 KJV*

❖❖❖❖❖❖❖❖❖❖❖❖❖❖❖❖❖❖❖❖❖❖❖❖❖❖❖❖❖❖❖❖❖❖❖❖❖❖❖❖❖❖❖❖❖❖

## A Prayer at Christmas

Father, Your gifts are priceless. You gave Your
Son Jesus, and Your motivation was love.
During this season of thanksgiving and
generosity, I pray that the gifts I give to others
will come from an overflow of my heart,
and that they will echo the great love
You have for all of Your children.

*Amen*

# Christmas Memories

I thank my God every time I remember you.
*—Philippians 1:3 NIV*

No season carries with it as many memories as the holiday season. As December 25th approaches, we are confronted with a double dose of memory-evoking events: the end of another year and the passing of another Christmas. No wonder we find ourselves reflecting on the past!

This year, as we celebrate this holiday season and give thanks for the ones who have gone before, let us thank God for *all* His blessings, past, present, and future. And let us keep our happy memories of Christmases past forever in our hearts.

*God gave us memories
that we might have roses
in December.*

—

SIR JAMES BARRIE

Happy, happy Christmas, that can win us back to the delusions of our childhood days, recall to the old man the pleasures of his youth, and transport the traveler back to his own fireside and quiet home!

—*Charles Dickens*

You remember hundreds of Christmas moments, and you laugh—or weep—with the dearest of them.

—*Margaret Lee Runbeck*

❖❖❖❖❖❖❖❖❖❖❖❖❖❖❖❖❖❖❖❖❖❖❖❖❖❖❖❖❖❖❖❖❖❖❖❖❖❖❖❖❖❖

*Christmas, my child, is always.*

—

DALE EVANS

❖❖❖❖❖❖❖❖❖❖❖❖❖❖❖❖❖❖❖❖❖❖❖❖❖❖❖❖❖❖❖❖❖❖❖❖❖❖❖❖❖❖

## A Prayer at Christmas

Thank you, Heavenly Father,
for the treasured memories of
Christmases past and for the loved ones
who have graced my life. Help me
to make *this* Christmas season
a memorable celebration of
the birth of Your Son.

## Amen

# Celebrating God's Grace

For it is by grace you have been saved, through faith—and this not from yourselves, it is the gift of God—not by works, so that no one can boast.

—*Ephesians 2:8-9 NIV*

As we gather our families together to celebrate the birth of Christ, we should consider the priceless gift of eternal life, a gift that is not earned by us, but one that is instead bestowed by God.

When we accept Christ into our lives, we are saved by God's grace. Let us praise God for His gift, and let us share His Good News today, throughout the holiday season, and every day that we live.

*All men who live with any degree of serenity live by some assurance of grace.*

—

REINHOLD NIEBUHR

This is Christmas, the real meaning of it: God loving, searching, giving Himself to us; man needing, receiving, giving himself to God. Redemption's glorious exchange of gifts, without which we cannot live, without which we cannot give to those we love anything of lasting value. This is the meaning of Christmas, the wonder and the glory of it.

—*Ruth Bell Graham*

The supreme force in salvation is God's grace. Not our works. Not our talents. Not our feelings. Not our strength.

—*Max Lucado*

For all have sinned and fall short of the glory of God, and are justified freely by his grace through the redemption that came by Christ Jesus.

—*Romans 3:23-24 NIV*

❋

He said unto me, My grace is sufficient for thee: for my strength is made perfect in weakness.

—*2 Corinthians 12:9 KJV*

# A Prayer at Christmas

Father, You have saved me by Your grace.
Keep me mindful that Your grace is a gift
that I can accept but cannot earn. I praise
You for that priceless gift, today, tomorrow,
and forever. Let me share the good news
of Your grace with a world that desperately
needs Your healing touch.

*Amen*

# A Time for Worship

I was glad when they said unto me, Let us go into the house of the LORD.

—*Psalm 122:1 KJV*

*C*hristmas should be, first and fore-most, a time to worship God and to give thanks for the gift of His Son. When we worship God, either alone or in the company of fellow believers, we are blessed. But when we fail to worship God, for whatever reason, we forfeit the spiritual riches that are rightfully ours.

Every day provides opportunities to put God where He belongs: at the center of our lives. Let us worship Him, and only Him, today and always.

There is no division into sacred and secular; it is all one great, glorious life.

—*Oswald Chambers*

Worship is not taught from the pulpit. It must be learned in the heart.

—*Jim Elliot*

The fact that we were created to enjoy God and to worship him forever is etched upon our souls.

—*Jim Cymbala*

A sense of deity is inscribed on every heart.

—*John Calvin*

Because his spiritual existence transcends form, matter, and location, we have the freedom to worship him and experience his indwelling presence wherever we are.

—*R. C. Sproul*

Let this be your chief object in prayer: to realize the presence of your heavenly Father. Let your watchword be: Alone with God.

—*Andrew Murray*

*Be still, and know that*
*I am God....*

—

PSALM 46:10 KJV

In the sanctuary, we discover beauty: the beauty of His presence.

—*Kay Arthur*

Spiritual worship is focusing all we are on all He is.

—*Beth Moore*

Let us remember therefore this lesson: That to worship our God sincerely we must evermore begin by harkening to His voice, and by giving ear to what He commands us.

—*John Calvin*

Worship is a voluntary act of gratitude offered by the saved to the Savior, by the healed to the Healer, and by the delivered to the Deliverer.

—*Max Lucado*

❄

Don't ever come to church without coming as though it were the first time, as though it could be the best time, and as though it might be the last time.

—*Vance Havner*

❄

Blessed are they which do hunger and thirst after righteousness: for they shall be filled.

—*Matthew 5:6 KJV*

# A Prayer at Christmas

Lord, let Christmas day and every day be a
time of worship. Whether I am in Your house
or simply going about my daily activities,
let me worship You, not only with words
and deeds, but also with my heart.
In my quiet moments, let me praise You and
thank You for creating me, for loving me,
for guiding me, and for saving me.

## Amen

# Joy to the World

Rejoice, and be exceeding glad: for great
is your reward in heaven . . . .

—*Matthew 5:12 KJV*

*C*hrist made it clear to His followers: He intended that His joy would become their joy. And it still holds true today: Christ intends that His believers share His love, His peace, His abundance, and His joy.

This Christmas season let us gladly accept the joy that is ours through Jesus Christ. Then, with thanksgiving in our hearts, we can gather together like the shepherds of old and praise the newborn babe, the humble Christ child, the Savior of the world.

❖❖❖❖❖❖❖❖❖❖❖❖❖❖❖❖❖❖❖❖❖❖❖❖❖❖❖❖❖❖❖❖❖❖❖❖❖❖❖❖❖❖❖❖❖

God can take any man and put the miracle of His joy into him.

*—Oswald Chambers*

O the precious name of Jesus! How it thrills our souls with joy.

*—Lydia Baxter*

There is not one blade of grass, there is no color in this world that is not intended to make us rejoice.

*—John Calvin*

❖❖❖❖❖❖❖❖❖❖❖❖❖❖❖❖❖❖❖❖❖❖❖❖❖❖❖❖❖❖❖❖❖❖❖❖❖❖❖❖❖❖❖❖❖

*Joy to the world!*
*The Lord is come!*
*Let earth receive her king;*

*let every heart prepare Him room,*
*and heaven and nature sing,*
*and heaven and nature sing,*
*and heaven, and heaven,*
*and nature sing.*

—

ISAAC WATTS, 1719

*The heavens declare the glory of God; and the firmament showeth his handiwork.*

—

PSALM 19:1 KJV

*Christmas waves a magic wand over the world, and, behold, everything is softer and more beautiful.*

—

NORMAN VINCENT PEALE

*It came upon
the midnight clear,
that glorious song of old,
From angels bending
near the earth,
to touch their harps of gold.*

*Peace on the earth,*
*goodwill to men,*
*from heav'n's all gracious king,*
*The world in solemn stillness*
*lay to hear the angels sing.*

—

EDMUND SEARS, 1850

*M*ay we not
"spend" Christmas or
"observe" Christmas,
but rather "keep" it.

—

PETER MARSHALL

Christmas is about a baby, born in a stable, who changed the world forever.

—*John Maxwell*

Christmas is the gift from heaven of God's Son, given for free. If Christmas isn't found in your heart, you won't find it under the tree.

—*Charlotte Carpenter*

At Christmas, surroundings do not matter because the spirit of Jesus is everywhere, knocking on the doors of our hearts.

—*Norman Vincent Peale*

The Lord is glad to open the gate to every knocking soul. It opens very freely; its hinges are not rusted; no bolts secure it. Have faith and enter at this moment through holy courage. If you knock with a heavy heart, you shall yet sing with joy of spirit.

—*C. H. Spurgeon*

Rejoice, the Lord is King; Your Lord and King adore! Rejoice, give thanks and sing and triumph evermore.

—*Charles Wesley*

The gloom of the world is but a shadow. Behind it, yet within reach, is joy. There is radiance and glory in the darkness, could we but see, and to see, we have only to look.

—*Fra Giovanni*

Claim the joy that is yours. Pray. And know that your joy is used by God to reach others.

—*Kay Arthur*

❄

Christ is not only a remedy for your weariness and trouble, but he will give you an abundance of the contrary: joy and delight.

—*Jonathan Edwards*

*Joy is the characteristic by which God uses us to re-make the distressing into the desired, the discarded into the creative. Joy is prayer—joy is strength— joy is love—joy is a net of love by which you can catch souls.*

—

MOTHER TERESA

*Joyful, joyful, we adore thee,
God of glory, Lord of love.
Hearts unfold like
flowers before thee;
opening to the sun above.*

—

HENRY VAN DYKE

*The Christmas spirit—
love—
changes hearts and lives.*

—

PAT BOONE

I will give you a new heart and put a new
spirit in you . . . .

*—Ezekiel 36:26 NIV*

❄

Therefore if any man be in Christ, he is a
new creature: old things are passed away; behold,
all things are become new.

*—2 Corinthians 5:17 KJV*

❄

He restoreth my soul.

*—Psalm 23:3 KJV*

*Go tell it on the mountain,*
*over the hills and everywhere.*
*Go tell it on the mountain,*
*that Jesus Christ is born!*

—

TRADITIONAL SPIRITUAL

*Y*ou are the God who performs
miracles . . . .

—

PSALM 77:14 NIV

*Hark! the herald angels sing,
"Glory to the newborn King."
Peace on earth and mercy mild;
God and sinners reconciled.
Joyful all ye nations rise.*

*Join the triumph of the skies;*
*with angelic host proclaim,*
*"Christ is born in Bethlehem!"*
*Hark! The herald angels sing,*
*"Glory to the newborn King."*

—

CHARLES WESLEY

*What child is this,*
*Who, laid to rest,*
*on Mary's lap is sleeping?*
*Whom angels greet*
*with anthems sweet,*
*while shepherds*
*watch are keeping?*

*This, this is Christ the King,*
*Whom shepherds guard*
*and angels sing.*
*Haste, haste*
*to bring Him laud,*
*the Babe,*
*the Son of Mary.*

—

WILLIAM C. DIX

*I truly believe that if we keep telling the Christmas story, singing the Christmas songs, and living the Christmas spirit, we can bring joy and happiness and peace to this world.*

—

NORMAN VINCENT PEALE

*These things have I spoken
unto you, that my joy might
remain in you, and that
your joy might be full.*

—

JOHN 15:11 KJV

## A Prayer at Christmas

Lord, make me a joyful Christian,
not just on Christmas day, but every day
of the year. Let me tell the story of
Your Son, not just at Christmastime,
but in every season of the year.
Let me be Your generous,
loving, faithful servant, today,
tomorrow, and forever.

## Amen